my
travel adventures

THIS BOOK BELONGS TO

....

only sleep once more

THAT IS WHERE WE ARE TRAVELING THIS TIME:
_____
_____
_____
_____

THEN STARTS OUR TRIP
_____
_____

THEN WE COME BACK
_____

I REALLY WANT TO EXPERIENCE THAT:

I LOOK FORWARD TO THAT:

I DON'T WANT TO DO THAT:

This is how I envision our vacation trip

I pack my suitcase and this comes with

Have I forgotten anything ?

Finally we are off

We will travel with (please tick)

That's how many miles
we travel (my parents say)

. . . .

THAT'S HOW MANY HOURS
WE WILL BE ON THE ROAD.
(FOR EACH HOUR
ONE POINT.)

AS LONG AS WE WERE
REALLY ON THE WAY
(MARKS FOR EACH HOUR
A POINT.)

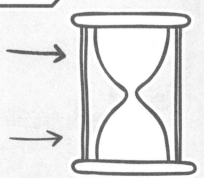

I'm so bored...

IF YOU ARE REALLY THAT BORED, THEN

WRITE DOWN ALL THE CITIES
THAT YOU WILL PASS:

THIS CITY HAD THE
FUNNIEST NAME

COUNT IT:

CARS YOU HAVE PASSED . . . .

PEE BREAKS . . . .

TUNNEL . . . .

BRIDGES . . . .

PETROL STATIONS . . . .

ANIMALS . . . .

WITH THIS WE CAN PASS THE BOREDOM

- [ ] NAME, PLACE, ANIMAL, THING
- [ ] GUESS CAR LICENSE PLATE
- [ ] CAN YOU SEE WHAT I SEE
- [ ] GUESS ANIMAL SOUNDS

DRAW A PICTURE OF HOW IT LOOKS LIKE AT YOUR PLACE RIGHT NOW.

U	Y	A	S	V	D	S	E	Y	A
C	E	L	B	R	X	W	P	R	B
T	R	K	I	K	L	T	N	M	K
S	A	B	K	D	O	G	T	O	Q
J	B	R	M	T	B	F	J	N	N
X	B	P	H	S	L	C	R	K	R
R	I	Z	M	L	Z	N	B	E	O
P	T	X	H	D	G	Z	P	Y	I
G	I	R	W	P	C	A	T	Q	Z
W	K	G	B	O	Z	J	B	G	B

BIRD
DOG
RABBIT

CAT
MONKEY

U	L	U	M	Q	M	B	Y	Y	N
S	C	A	T	O	S	L	K	M	I
V	V	V	I	B	H	D	T	K	Y
C	K	K	Q	A	E	O	A	W	I
N	P	A	B	F	E	G	E	S	U
I	J	N	E	F	P	S	I	Q	Y
U	E	P	I	T	R	V	Z	P	V
N	C	Y	Z	O	R	S	M	V	N
N	I	D	H	L	X	X	X	Y	Z
D	M	A	R	A	B	B	I	T	K

CAT
HORSE
SHEEP

DOG
RABBIT

J	W	G	W	D	E	L	F	G	K
A	Z	R	C	J	H	G	O	O	E
V	A	C	A	T	I	O	N	J	J
C	Y	L	P	O	O	L	N	B	I
H	S	X	N	Z	J	U	Q	R	K
E	R	N	L	F	S	W	D	Z	G
Q	F	H	O	L	I	D	A	Y	T
Q	B	C	A	R	A	V	A	N	N
M	T	Z	K	S	P	L	H	O	L
U	I	T	Q	M	S	U	C	X	E

CARAVAN
POOL
VACATION

HOLIDAY
SUN

R	U	Z	V	K	B	T	D	U	E
C	W	E	H	B	J	W	Q	N	G
R	C	I	A	U	N	Z	O	N	X
S	K	P	D	C	M	T	I	W	S
C	M	R	T	K	S	W	R	H	Z
H	J	B	R	E	S	Q	T	Y	B
W	E	P	E	T	C	Y	N	B	C
J	Q	H	E	A	D	N	O	E	I
B	U	C	L	I	M	B	I	N	G
Z	W	H	D	X	H	H	O	T	I

BUCKET
STONE
TREE

CLIMBING
SWING

1

7	6						8	9
	9		7	6				1
	1	8	4			5		
				7		2		4
	7	1	2	9	4			
		4	3	1				8
				4	3	7		
9			6		1		5	3
5		6				1		

2

7							5	3
6				2		4		
		4		6	1			
			2	3	4			1
	9	8			7			
			5			3	6	7
	6			5			9	2
1		3	8			5		
9	8		4	7	2	1		

3

9	5	7		1				
						1	7	3
			6	8	7	9	2	
			3		5	2	6	
		2		9		5		
	1	5			8			
	6		7				3	9
5				6		7		
1	7		9					4

4

7	4	1				2		
		9		5		1	3	8
			1	6	2			
6	9		7		5	4		
		4	6			9		5
5		7		1	4			
	7		3					1
			5	9		3		
	1	8					9	4

5

3	4	8	6		1			
		9	3	5	2			
						6	3	7
				2	3			
	9		8			1	7	3
	3	7			5		8	
4			9	1		2		8
2	7			6				4
9				3	4			

6

						8	6	4
	7	3			5			
1		4		2	9			7
			5			4		
	5		1		8	9	7	
9	4			3			1	5
			3	9	1			6
2	1	7						
	9		2			5		

7

	9				6		7	
	7					3	2	
	1		8			4		5
			1		8	7	6	2
7		1	6	2			5	4
		4	9					
5					9		4	7
			2	8				
2	3	9				5		1

8

6	7	5		1		9		
	9					1	2	3
			4	8				
7	3		9	4				
1			7			4	3	
4			2	5			1	
	1	3			7			2
2		7						1
		8			2		7	5

9

		6	4		1			
		5	9				2	
		3			6	4	9	
1	8				5	7		
9	3		1			5	4	8
			2	4				1
7	2					8	5	
5		1		3		2		
3					7			

10

6	3			5				8
9					6	7		5
			9		7		1	6
				6		8		4
5	2	3				1		
			1	7	5	9		
	5	1				6	2	
		2		3	9		7	
		6	5		2			

11

			1			3		2
2	1	9			6	8		
4	6				7			
	2	1	6				4	
			7	3				9
		4			2	7	8	
3	7		6			2		8
8	4		5		3		1	
			8					5

12

5							8	
3				6	4	9		2
6	1			2	8	5	7	
		3	2					6
	6	7	8			2		
		2	7			1	3	9
	8	6					5	
	3					7		4
			3	1	9	6		

13

```
. . 2 | 3 . . | 1 . 5
4 2 . | . 6 9 | 3 . .
9 . . | . . . | 6 . 4
------+-------+------
. . . | 1 8 . | . 4 2
. 8 1 | . . 5 | . . .
. . 6 | 3 . 2 | . 8 .
------+-------+------
1 . . | . . . | 4 . 6
. 7 . | 8 5 . | . 3 .
5 3 . | 9 4 . | . . .
```

14

```
6 . 3 | . 2 4 | 7 . .
. . 8 | 1 . 5 | 6 . 2
4 . . | 9 . 7 | . . 8
------+-------+------
. . . | 5 2 . | . . 6
. 4 . | . . 1 | 8 5 .
. 1 . | 6 . . | 4 . .
------+-------+------
5 . 2 | . 9 . | . 8 .
8 . . | . . 6 | . 7 5
. . 9 | 5 . . | . . .
```

15

```
. . 3 | . . 8 | 7 . 6
. . . | 9 6 . | . 3 1
7 4 6 | . . . | . . 9
------+-------+------
. 1 . | 2 9 . | . . 8
2 7 . | . 1 . | . 4 3
. 8 4 | . . 5 | . . .
------+-------+------
8 . . | . 9 . | . . .
9 . 1 | 7 . . | 4 3 .
. . . | 1 . . | 8 6 .
```

16

```
. 4 . | . 9 6 | . 2 7
2 . 9 | . . 5 | . . .
. . 5 | . . 7 | . . 9
------+-------+------
8 6 . | . 2 . | . 1 .
. 2 . | 7 5 . | . 3 .
5 . . | . 1 3 | 8 4 .
------+-------+------
. . . | 3 . . | 4 7 8
7 . . | . 4 . | . . .
9 . . | . 4 . | 2 . 3
```

17

```
4 . 1 | 3 6 . | . . .
6 . . | 2 5 . | . 9 .
. 5 3 | . 1 . | . 4 2
------+-------+------
5 . 6 | 4 . 7 | . . .
. 4 . | . . . | 3 2 5
1 8 2 | 9 . . | . 6 4
------+-------+------
. . . | . . 1 | 9 . 8
. . . | 6 7 3 | 2 . .
3 1 5 | . . . | . . .
```

18

```
. . 2 | 1 6 7 | . . 5
. 5 . | . . . | . 1 9
. 1 . | . . . | 7 . 2
------+-------+------
9 . 4 | . . 1 | . 7 .
6 . . | . . . | . 8 .
3 . . | . 2 9 | . . 6
------+-------+------
. 4 . | 2 7 . | 5 . .
. 7 . | . 1 . | 6 . 4
. 8 6 | 4 . . | . 9 .
```

19

	2	8		6				
		7		4		5	6	
				1	7	8	4	
6		5			2		7	
8					6		5	4
2			4		3			
5			6			4	1	
			5			9		8
	8	3	7		4			

20

	3			7				
					4			8
9	4			2	8		6	
	6		7	1		5		
5			8	4		6	7	
4	8		5			3		1
7	1	3					4	
		4			6		9	3
		6	4				1	

21

	2	4			9			
		6	3			1	8	
		3		7	6	5		
	7		6	9		4	3	1
4	5					6	2	
			8	2	4			
				3				7
8			2	6				9
9		2		4				6

22

				6			3	8
		3	9	1		6		
6		7		8				
4	2		1			9		
	1		3		8			7
7						1	4	5
1			4		2	7		
9	7					5	2	1
3		2					9	4

23

7				2	5			
		9			4	8	2	3
4		8					1	
			1	3	6			
9		3	4	8			5	
	1			6		4		7
	9		7					1
1	7		6		2			9
		2	9			3		6

24

9	3	2						
	1			4			5	3
	5			3	8		7	
		1			2	9	8	4
	9		3					2
2			7		4			
			5			4		
5			4	1	3	6		
7		6	8				3	

DATE: . . . .

LOCATION: . . . .

. . . .

WEATHER 🌡 . . . °F

THAT'S WHAT I EXPERIENCED TODAY:

. . . .

. . . .

. . . .

THAT'S WHAT I SEEN TODAY:

. . . .

. . . .

. . . .

THIS IS WHAT I ATE TODAY:

. . . .

. . . .

. . . .

DRAW WHAT YOU HAVE EXPERIENCED TODAY:

OR INSERT PHOTOS, ENTRY CARDS OR STAMPS

MY FAVORITE MEMORY TODAY

. . . .

. . . .

I AM GRATEFUL FOR THAT TODAY

. . . .

. . . .

THIS IS HOW MY DAY WAS TODAY

DATE: . . . .

WEATHER 🌡 . . . °F

LOCATION: . . . .

THAT'S WHAT I EXPERIENCED TODAY:

. . . .

. . . .

. . . .

THAT'S WHAT I SEEN TODAY:

. . . .

. . . .

. . . .

THIS IS WHAT I ATE TODAY:

. . . .

. . . .

. . . .

DRAW WHAT YOU HAVE EXPERIENCED TODAY:

OR INSERT PHOTOS, ENTRY CARDS OR STAMPS

MY FAVORITE MEMORY TODAY

. . . .

. . . .

I AM GRATEFUL FOR THAT TODAY

. . . .

. . . .

THIS IS HOW MY DAY WAS TODAY

DATE: . . . .

WEATHER 🌡 . . . °F

LOCATION: . . . .

. . . .

THAT'S WHAT I EXPERIENCED TODAY:

. . . .

. . . .

. . . .

THAT'S WHAT I SEEN TODAY:

. . . .

. . . .

. . . .

THIS IS WHAT I ATE TODAY:

. . . .

. . . .

. . . .

DRAW WHAT YOU HAVE EXPERIENCED TODAY:

OR INSERT PHOTOS, ENTRY CARDS OR STAMPS

MY FAVORITE MEMORY TODAY

. . . .

. . . .

I AM GRATEFUL FOR THAT TODAY

. . . .

. . . .

THIS IS HOW MY DAY WAS TODAY

DATE: . . . .

WEATHER 🌡️ . . . . °F

LOCATION: . . . .

THAT'S WHAT I EXPERIENCED TODAY:

. . . .

. . . .

. . . .

THAT'S WHAT I SEEN TODAY:

. . . .

. . . .

. . . .

THIS IS WHAT I ATE TODAY:

. . . .

. . . .

. . . .

DRAW WHAT YOU HAVE EXPERIENCED TODAY:

OR INSERT PHOTOS, ENTRY CARDS OR STAMPS

MY FAVORITE MEMORY TODAY

. . . .

. . . .

I AM GRATEFUL FOR THAT TODAY

. . . .

. . . .

THIS IS HOW MY DAY WAS TODAY

DATE: . . . .

WEATHER . . . . °F

LOCATION: . . . .

THAT'S WHAT I EXPERIENCED TODAY:

. . . .

. . . .

. . . .

THAT'S WHAT I SEEN TODAY:

. . . .

. . . .

. . . .

THIS IS WHAT I ATE TODAY:

. . . .

. . . .

. . . .

DRAW WHAT YOU HAVE EXPERIENCED TODAY:

OR INSERT PHOTOS, ENTRY CARDS OR STAMPS

MY FAVORITE MEMORY TODAY

. . . .

. . . .

I AM GRATEFUL FOR THAT TODAY

. . . .

. . . .

THIS IS HOW MY DAY WAS TODAY

DATE: . . . .

WEATHER 🌡 . . . . °F

LOCATION: . . . .

THAT'S WHAT I EXPERIENCED TODAY:

. . . .

. . . .

. . . .

THAT'S WHAT I SEEN TODAY:

. . . .

. . . .

. . . .

THIS IS WHAT I ATE TODAY:

. . . .

. . . .

. . . .

DRAW WHAT YOU HAVE EXPERIENCED TODAY:

OR INSERT PHOTOS, ENTRY CARDS OR STAMPS

MY FAVORITE MEMORY TODAY

. . . .

. . . .

I AM GRATEFUL FOR THAT TODAY

. . . .

. . . .

THIS IS HOW MY DAY WAS TODAY

DATE: . . . .

WEATHER 🌡 . . . . °F

LOCATION: . . . .

THAT'S WHAT I EXPERIENCED TODAY:

. . . .

. . . .

. . . .

THAT'S WHAT I SEEN TODAY:

. . . .

. . . .

. . . .

THIS IS WHAT I ATE TODAY:

. . . .

. . . .

. . . .

DRAW WHAT YOU HAVE EXPERIENCED TODAY:

OR INSERT PHOTOS, ENTRY CARDS OR STAMPS

MY FAVORITE MEMORY TODAY

. . . .

. . . .

I AM GRATEFUL FOR THAT TODAY

. . . .

. . . .

THIS IS HOW MY DAY WAS TODAY

DATE: . . . .

LOCATION: . . . .

WEATHER . . . . °F

THAT'S WHAT I EXPERIENCED TODAY:

. . . .

. . . .

. . . .

THAT'S WHAT I SEEN TODAY:

. . . .

. . . .

. . . .

THIS IS WHAT I ATE TODAY:

. . . .

. . . .

. . . .

DRAW WHAT YOU HAVE EXPERIENCED TODAY:

OR INSERT PHOTOS, ENTRY CARDS OR STAMPS

MY FAVORITE MEMORY TODAY

. . . .

. . . .

I AM GRATEFUL FOR THAT TODAY

. . . .

. . . .

THIS IS HOW MY DAY WAS TODAY

DATE: . . . .

WEATHER 🌡 . . . °F

LOCATION: . . . .

THAT'S WHAT I EXPERIENCED TODAY:

. . . .

. . . .

. . . .

THAT'S WHAT I SEEN TODAY:

. . . .

. . . .

. . . .

THIS IS WHAT I ATE TODAY:

. . . .

. . . .

. . . .

DRAW WHAT YOU HAVE EXPERIENCED TODAY:

OR INSERT PHOTOS, ENTRY CARDS OR STAMPS

MY FAVORITE MEMORY TODAY

. . . .

. . . .

I AM GRATEFUL FOR THAT TODAY

. . . .

. . . .

THIS IS HOW MY DAY WAS TODAY

DATE: . . . .

WEATHER 🌡 . . . . . °F

LOCATION: . . . .

THAT'S WHAT I EXPERIENCED TODAY:

. . . .

. . . .

. . . .

THAT'S WHAT I SEEN TODAY:

. . . .

. . . .

. . . .

THIS IS WHAT I ATE TODAY:

. . . .

. . . .

. . . .

DRAW WHAT YOU HAVE EXPERIENCED TODAY:

OR INSERT PHOTOS, ENTRY CARDS OR STAMPS

MY FAVORITE MEMORY TODAY

· ·

· ·

I AM GRATEFUL FOR THAT TODAY

· ·

· ·

THIS IS HOW MY DAY WAS TODAY

DATE: . . . .

WEATHER 🌡️ . . . °F

LOCATION:
📍 . . . .
. . . .

THAT'S WHAT I EXPERIENCED TODAY:

. . . .

. . . .

. . . .

THAT'S WHAT I SEEN TODAY:

. . . .

. . . .

. . . .

THIS IS WHAT I ATE TODAY:

. . . .

. . . .

. . . .

DRAW WHAT YOU HAVE EXPERIENCED TODAY:

OR INSERT PHOTOS, ENTRY CARDS OR STAMPS

MY FAVORITE MEMORY TODAY

. . . .

. . . .

I AM GRATEFUL FOR THAT TODAY

. . . .

. . . .

THIS IS HOW MY DAY WAS TODAY

DATE: . . . .

WEATHER °F

LOCATION: . . . .

THAT'S WHAT I EXPERIENCED TODAY:

. . . .

. . . .

. . . .

THAT'S WHAT I SEEN TODAY:

. . . .

. . . .

. . . .

THIS IS WHAT I ATE TODAY:

. . . .

. . . .

. . . .

DRAW WHAT YOU HAVE EXPERIENCED TODAY:

OR INSERT PHOTOS, ENTRY CARDS OR STAMPS

MY FAVORITE MEMORY TODAY

. . . .

. . . .

I AM GRATEFUL FOR THAT TODAY

. . . .

. . . .

THIS IS HOW MY DAY WAS TODAY

DATE: . . . .

WEATHER 🌡 . . . °F

LOCATION: . . . .
. . . .

THAT'S WHAT I EXPERIENCED TODAY:

. . . .

. . . .

. . . .

THAT'S WHAT I SEEN TODAY:

. . . .

. . . .

. . . .

THIS IS WHAT I ATE TODAY:

. . . .

. . . .

. . . .

DRAW WHAT YOU HAVE EXPERIENCED TODAY:

OR INSERT PHOTOS, ENTRY CARDS OR STAMPS

MY FAVORITE MEMORY TODAY

. . . .

. . . .

I AM GRATEFUL FOR THAT TODAY

. . . .

. . . .

THIS IS HOW MY DAY WAS TODAY

DATE: . . . .

WEATHER 🌡 . . . . °F

LOCATION: . . . .

THAT'S WHAT I EXPERIENCED TODAY:

. . . .

. . . .

. . . .

THAT'S WHAT I SEEN TODAY:

. . . .

. . . .

. . . .

THIS IS WHAT I ATE TODAY:

. . . .

. . . .

. . . .

DRAW WHAT YOU HAVE EXPERIENCED TODAY:

OR INSERT PHOTOS, ENTRY CARDS OR STAMPS

MY FAVORITE MEMORY TODAY

. . . .

. . . .

I AM GRATEFUL FOR THAT TODAY

. . . .

. . . .

THIS IS HOW MY DAY WAS TODAY

DATE: . . . .

WEATHER 🌡 . . . °F

LOCATION: . . . .

THAT'S WHAT I EXPERIENCED TODAY:

. . . .

. . . .

. . . .

THAT'S WHAT I SEEN TODAY:

. . . .

. . . .

. . . .

THIS IS WHAT I ATE TODAY:

. . . .

. . . .

. . . .

DRAW WHAT YOU HAVE EXPERIENCED TODAY:

OR INSERT PHOTOS, ENTRY CARDS OR STAMPS

MY FAVORITE MEMORY TODAY

. . . .

. . . .

I AM GRATEFUL FOR THAT TODAY

. . . .

. . . .

THIS IS HOW MY DAY WAS TODAY

DATE: . . . .

WEATHER . . . . °F

LOCATION: . . . .

THAT'S WHAT I EXPERIENCED TODAY:

. . . .

. . . .

. . . .

THAT'S WHAT I SEEN TODAY:

. . . .

. . . .

. . . .

THIS IS WHAT I ATE TODAY:

. . . .

. . . .

. . . .

DRAW WHAT YOU HAVE EXPERIENCED TODAY:

OR INSERT PHOTOS, ENTRY CARDS OR STAMPS

MY FAVORITE MEMORY TODAY

. . . .

. . . .

I AM GRATEFUL FOR THAT TODAY

. . . .

. . . .

THIS IS HOW MY DAY WAS TODAY

DATE: . . . .

WEATHER 🌡 . . . **°F**

LOCATION: . . . .
. . . .

THAT'S WHAT I EXPERIENCED TODAY:

. . . .

. . . .

. . . .

THAT'S WHAT I SEEN TODAY:

. . . .

. . . .

. . . .

THIS IS WHAT I ATE TODAY:

. . . .

. . . .

. . . .

DRAW WHAT YOU HAVE EXPERIENCED TODAY:

OR INSERT PHOTOS, ENTRY CARDS OR STAMPS

MY FAVORITE MEMORY TODAY

. . . .

. . . .

I AM GRATEFUL FOR THAT TODAY

. . . .

. . . .

THIS IS HOW MY DAY WAS TODAY

DATE: . . . .

WEATHER 🌡 . . . °F

LOCATION: . . . .
. . . .

THAT'S WHAT I EXPERIENCED TODAY:

. . . .
. . . .
. . . .

THAT'S WHAT I SEEN TODAY:

. . . .
. . . .
. . . .

THIS IS WHAT I ATE TODAY:

. . . .
. . . .
. . . .

DRAW WHAT YOU HAVE EXPERIENCED TODAY:

OR INSERT PHOTOS, ENTRY CARDS OR STAMPS

MY FAVORITE MEMORY TODAY

. . . .

. . . .

I AM GRATEFUL FOR THAT TODAY

. . . .

. . . .

THIS IS HOW MY DAY WAS TODAY

DATE: . . . .

LOCATION: . . . .

WEATHER 🌡 . . . °F

THAT'S WHAT I EXPERIENCED TODAY:

. . . .

. . . .

. . . .

THAT'S WHAT I SEEN TODAY:

. . . .

. . . .

. . . .

THIS IS WHAT I ATE TODAY:

. . . .

. . . .

. . . .

DRAW WHAT YOU HAVE EXPERIENCED TODAY:

OR INSERT PHOTOS, ENTRY CARDS OR STAMPS

MY FAVORITE MEMORY TODAY

. . . .

. . . .

I AM GRATEFUL FOR THAT TODAY

. . . .

. . . .

THIS IS HOW MY DAY WAS TODAY

DATE: . . . .

WEATHER 🌡 . . . °F

LOCATION: . . . .

THAT'S WHAT I EXPERIENCED TODAY:

. . . .

. . . .

. . . .

THAT'S WHAT I SEEN TODAY:

. . . .

. . . .

. . . .

THIS IS WHAT I ATE TODAY:

. . . .

. . . .

. . . .

DRAW WHAT YOU HAVE EXPERIENCED TODAY:

OR INSERT PHOTOS, ENTRY CARDS OR STAMPS

MY FAVORITE MEMORY TODAY

. . . .

. . . .

I AM GRATEFUL FOR THAT TODAY

. . . .

. . . .

THIS IS HOW MY DAY WAS TODAY

DATE: . . . .

WEATHER 🌡 . . . °F

LOCATION: . . . .

THAT'S WHAT I EXPERIENCED TODAY:

. . . .

. . . .

. . . .

THAT'S WHAT I SEEN TODAY:

. . . .

. . . .

. . . .

THIS IS WHAT I ATE TODAY:

. . . .

. . . .

. . . .

DRAW WHAT YOU HAVE EXPERIENCED TODAY:

OR INSERT PHOTOS, ENTRY CARDS OR STAMPS

MY FAVORITE MEMORY TODAY

. . . .

. . . .

I AM GRATEFUL FOR THAT TODAY

. . . .

. . . .

THIS IS HOW MY DAY WAS TODAY

DATE: . . . .

LOCATION: . . . .

WEATHER . . . . . °F

THAT'S WHAT I EXPERIENCED TODAY:

. . . .

. . . .

. . . .

THAT'S WHAT I SEEN TODAY:

. . . .

. . . .

. . . .

THIS IS WHAT I ATE TODAY:

. . . .

. . . .

. . . .

DRAW WHAT YOU HAVE EXPERIENCED TODAY:

OR INSERT PHOTOS, ENTRY CARDS OR STAMPS

MY FAVORITE MEMORY TODAY

. . . .

. . . .

I AM GRATEFUL FOR THAT TODAY

. . . .

. . . .

THIS IS HOW MY DAY WAS TODAY

DATE: . . . .

WEATHER 🌡 °F

LOCATION: . . . .
. . . .

THAT'S WHAT I EXPERIENCED TODAY:

. . . .

. . . .

. . . .

THAT'S WHAT I SEEN TODAY:

. . . .

. . . .

. . . .

THIS IS WHAT I ATE TODAY:

. . . .

. . . .

. . . .

DRAW WHAT YOU HAVE EXPERIENCED TODAY:

OR INSERT PHOTOS, ENTRY CARDS OR STAMPS

MY FAVORITE MEMORY TODAY

. . . .

. . . .

I AM GRATEFUL FOR THAT TODAY

. . . .

. . . .

THIS IS HOW MY DAY WAS TODAY

DATE: . . . .

LOCATION: . . . .

WEATHER 🌡 . . . . °F

THAT'S WHAT I EXPERIENCED TODAY:

. . . .

. . . .

. . . .

THAT'S WHAT I SEEN TODAY:

. . . .

. . . .

. . . .

THIS IS WHAT I ATE TODAY:

. . . .

. . . .

. . . .

DRAW WHAT YOU HAVE EXPERIENCED TODAY:

OR INSERT PHOTOS, ENTRY CARDS OR STAMPS

MY FAVORITE MEMORY TODAY

. . . .

. . . .

I AM GRATEFUL FOR THAT TODAY

. . . .

. . . .

THIS IS HOW MY DAY WAS TODAY

DATE: . . . .

LOCATION: . . . .

. . . .

WEATHER . . . . °F

THAT'S WHAT I EXPERIENCED TODAY:

. . . .

. . . .

. . . .

THAT'S WHAT I SEEN TODAY:

. . . .

. . . .

. . . .

THIS IS WHAT I ATE TODAY:

. . . .

. . . .

. . . .

DRAW WHAT YOU HAVE EXPERIENCED TODAY:

OR INSERT PHOTOS, ENTRY CARDS OR STAMPS

MY FAVORITE MEMORY TODAY

. . . .

. . . .

I AM GRATEFUL FOR THAT TODAY

. . . .

. . . .

THIS IS HOW MY DAY WAS TODAY

DATE: . . . .

WEATHER 🌡 . . . °F

LOCATION: . . . .

THAT'S WHAT I EXPERIENCED TODAY:

. . . .

. . . .

. . . .

THAT'S WHAT I SEEN TODAY:

. . . .

. . . .

. . . .

THIS IS WHAT I ATE TODAY:

. . . .

. . . .

. . . .

DRAW WHAT YOU HAVE EXPERIENCED TODAY:

OR INSERT PHOTOS, ENTRY CARDS OR STAMPS

MY FAVORITE MEMORY TODAY

. . . .

. . . .

I AM GRATEFUL FOR THAT TODAY

. . . .

. . . .

THIS IS HOW MY DAY WAS TODAY

DATE: . . . .

WEATHER °F

LOCATION: . . . .

THAT'S WHAT I EXPERIENCED TODAY:

. . . .

. . . .

. . . .

THAT'S WHAT I SEEN TODAY:

. . . .

. . . .

. . . .

THIS IS WHAT I ATE TODAY:

. . . .

. . . .

. . . .

DRAW WHAT YOU HAVE EXPERIENCED TODAY:

OR INSERT PHOTOS, ENTRY CARDS OR STAMPS

MY FAVORITE MEMORY TODAY

. . . .

. . . .

I AM GRATEFUL FOR THAT TODAY

. . . .

. . . .

THIS IS HOW MY DAY WAS TODAY

DATE: . . . .

WEATHER 🌡 . . . °F

LOCATION: . . . .

THAT'S WHAT I EXPERIENCED TODAY:

. . . .

. . . .

. . . .

THAT'S WHAT I SEEN TODAY:

. . . .

. . . .

. . . .

THIS IS WHAT I ATE TODAY:

. . . .

. . . .

. . . .

DRAW WHAT YOU HAVE EXPERIENCED TODAY:

OR INSERT PHOTOS, ENTRY CARDS OR STAMPS

MY FAVORITE MEMORY TODAY

. . . .

. . . .

I AM GRATEFUL FOR THAT TODAY

. . . .

. . . .

THIS IS HOW MY DAY WAS TODAY

  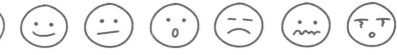

DATE:

LOCATION:

WEATHER °F

THAT'S WHAT I EXPERIENCED TODAY:

THAT'S WHAT I SEEN TODAY:

THIS IS WHAT I ATE TODAY:

DRAW WHAT YOU HAVE EXPERIENCED TODAY:

OR INSERT PHOTOS, ENTRY CARDS OR STAMPS

MY FAVORITE MEMORY TODAY

. . . .

. . . .

I AM GRATEFUL FOR THAT TODAY

. . . .

. . . .

THIS IS HOW MY DAY WAS TODAY

DATE: . . . .

WEATHER 🌡️ . . . °F

LOCATION:
📍 . . . .

THAT'S WHAT I EXPERIENCED TODAY:

. . . .

. . . .

. . . .

THAT'S WHAT I SEEN TODAY:

. . . .

. . . .

. . . .

THIS IS WHAT I ATE TODAY:

. . . .

. . . .

. . . .

DRAW WHAT YOU HAVE EXPERIENCED TODAY:

OR INSERT PHOTOS, ENTRY CARDS OR STAMPS

MY FAVORITE MEMORY TODAY

. . . .

. . . .

I AM GRATEFUL FOR THAT TODAY

. . . .

. . . .

THIS IS HOW MY DAY WAS TODAY

DATE: . . . .

WEATHER 🌡️ °F

LOCATION: . . . .
. . . .

THAT'S WHAT I EXPERIENCED TODAY:

. . . .

. . . .

. . . .

THAT'S WHAT I SEEN TODAY:

. . . .

. . . .

. . . .

THIS IS WHAT I ATE TODAY:

. . . .

. . . .

. . . .

DRAW WHAT YOU HAVE EXPERIENCED TODAY:

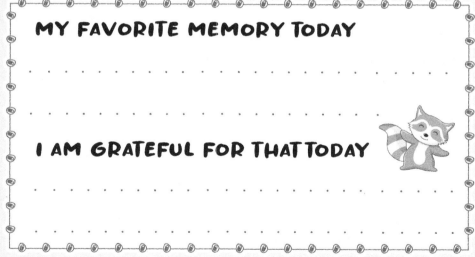

OR INSERT PHOTOS, ENTRY CARDS OR STAMPS

MY FAVORITE MEMORY TODAY

. . . .

. . . .

I AM GRATEFUL FOR THAT TODAY

. . . .

. . . .

THIS IS HOW MY DAY WAS TODAY

DATE: . . . .

WEATHER . . . °F

LOCATION: . . . .

THAT'S WHAT I EXPERIENCED TODAY:

. . . .

. . . .

. . . .

THAT'S WHAT I SEEN TODAY:

. . . .

. . . .

. . . .

THIS IS WHAT I ATE TODAY:

. . . .

. . . .

. . . .

DRAW WHAT YOU HAVE EXPERIENCED TODAY:

OR INSERT PHOTOS, ENTRY CARDS OR STAMPS

MY FAVORITE MEMORY TODAY

. . . .

. . . .

I AM GRATEFUL FOR THAT TODAY

. . . .

. . . .

THIS IS HOW MY DAY WAS TODAY

DATE: . . . .

WEATHER °F

LOCATION: . . . .

. . . .

THAT'S WHAT I EXPERIENCED TODAY:

. . . .

. . . .

. . . .

THAT'S WHAT I SEEN TODAY:

. . . .

. . . .

. . . .

THIS IS WHAT I ATE TODAY:

. . . .

. . . .

. . . .

DRAW WHAT YOU HAVE EXPERIENCED TODAY:

OR INSERT PHOTOS, ENTRY CARDS OR STAMPS

MY FAVORITE MEMORY TODAY

. . . .

. . . .

I AM GRATEFUL FOR THAT TODAY

. . . .

. . . .

THIS IS HOW MY DAY WAS TODAY

DATE: . . . .

WEATHER 🌡️ . . . °F

LOCATION:
📍 . . . .

. . . .

THAT'S WHAT I EXPERIENCED TODAY:

. . . .

. . . .

. . . .

THAT'S WHAT I SEEN TODAY:

. . . .

. . . .

. . . .

THIS IS WHAT I ATE TODAY:

. . . .

. . . .

. . . .

DRAW WHAT YOU HAVE EXPERIENCED TODAY:

OR INSERT PHOTOS, ENTRY CARDS OR STAMPS

MY FAVORITE MEMORY TODAY

. . . .

. . . .

I AM GRATEFUL FOR THAT TODAY

. . . .

. . . .

THIS IS HOW MY DAY WAS TODAY

DATE: . . . .

WEATHER 🌡 . . . °F

LOCATION: . . . .
. . . .

THAT'S WHAT I EXPERIENCED TODAY:

. . . .

. . . .

. . . .

THAT'S WHAT I SEEN TODAY:

. . . .

. . . .

. . . .

THIS IS WHAT I ATE TODAY:

. . . .

. . . .

. . . .

DRAW WHAT YOU HAVE EXPERIENCED TODAY:

OR INSERT PHOTOS, ENTRY CARDS OR STAMPS

MY FAVORITE MEMORY TODAY

· ·

· ·

I AM GRATEFUL FOR THAT TODAY

· ·

· ·

THIS IS HOW MY DAY WAS TODAY

DATE: . . . .

LOCATION: . . . .

WEATHER . . . °F

THAT'S WHAT I EXPERIENCED TODAY:

. . . .

THAT'S WHAT I SEEN TODAY:

. . . .

THIS IS WHAT I ATE TODAY:

. . . .

DRAW WHAT YOU HAVE EXPERIENCED TODAY:

OR INSERT PHOTOS, ENTRY CARDS OR STAMPS

MY FAVORITE MEMORY TODAY

. . . .

. . . .

I AM GRATEFUL FOR THAT TODAY

. . . .

. . . .

THIS IS HOW MY DAY WAS TODAY

DATE: . . . .

WEATHER 🌡 . . . °F

LOCATION: . . . .

THAT'S WHAT I EXPERIENCED TODAY:

. . . .

. . . .

. . . .

THAT'S WHAT I SEEN TODAY:

. . . .

. . . .

. . . .

THIS IS WHAT I ATE TODAY:

. . . .

. . . .

. . . .

DRAW WHAT YOU HAVE EXPERIENCED TODAY:

OR INSERT PHOTOS, ENTRY CARDS OR STAMPS

MY FAVORITE MEMORY TODAY

. . . .

. . . .

I AM GRATEFUL FOR THAT TODAY

. . . .

. . . .

THIS IS HOW MY DAY WAS TODAY

DATE: . . . .

WEATHER . . . . °F

LOCATION: . . . .

THAT'S WHAT I EXPERIENCED TODAY:

. . . .

. . . .

. . . .

THAT'S WHAT I SEEN TODAY:

. . . .

. . . .

. . . .

THIS IS WHAT I ATE TODAY:

. . . .

. . . .

. . . .

DRAW WHAT YOU HAVE EXPERIENCED TODAY:

OR INSERT PHOTOS, ENTRY CARDS OR STAMPS

MY FAVORITE MEMORY TODAY

. . . .

. . . .

I AM GRATEFUL FOR THAT TODAY

. . . .

. . . .

THIS IS HOW MY DAY WAS TODAY

DATE: . . . .

WEATHER 🌡 . . . °F

LOCATION: . . . .

THAT'S WHAT I EXPERIENCED TODAY:

. . . .

. . . .

. . . .

THAT'S WHAT I SEEN TODAY:

. . . .

. . . .

. . . .

THIS IS WHAT I ATE TODAY:

. . . .

. . . .

. . . .

DRAW WHAT YOU HAVE EXPERIENCED TODAY:

OR INSERT PHOTOS, ENTRY CARDS OR STAMPS

MY FAVORITE MEMORY TODAY

. . . .

. . . .

I AM GRATEFUL FOR THAT TODAY

. . . .

. . . .

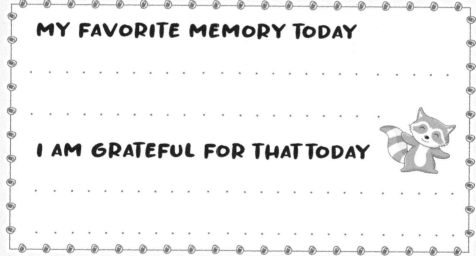

THIS IS HOW MY DAY WAS TODAY

DATE: . . . .

WEATHER 🌡 . . . °F

LOCATION: . . . .

THAT'S WHAT I EXPERIENCED TODAY:

. . . .

. . . .

. . . .

THAT'S WHAT I SEEN TODAY:

. . . .

. . . .

. . . .

THIS IS WHAT I ATE TODAY:

. . . .

. . . .

. . . .

DRAW WHAT YOU HAVE EXPERIENCED TODAY:

OR INSERT PHOTOS, ENTRY CARDS OR STAMPS

MY FAVORITE MEMORY TODAY

. . . .

. . . .

I AM GRATEFUL FOR THAT TODAY

. . . .

. . . .

THIS IS HOW MY DAY WAS TODAY

DATE: . . . .

LOCATION: . . . .

WEATHER . . . . °F

THAT'S WHAT I EXPERIENCED TODAY:

. . . .

. . . .

. . . .

THAT'S WHAT I SEEN TODAY:

. . . .

. . . .

. . . .

THIS IS WHAT I ATE TODAY:

. . . .

. . . .

. . . .

DRAW WHAT YOU HAVE EXPERIENCED TODAY:

OR INSERT PHOTOS, ENTRY CARDS OR STAMPS

MY FAVORITE MEMORY TODAY

. . . .

. . . .

I AM GRATEFUL FOR THAT TODAY

. . . .

. . . .

THIS IS HOW MY DAY WAS TODAY

DATE: . . . .

LOCATION: . . . .

WEATHER °F

THAT'S WHAT I EXPERIENCED TODAY:

. . . .

. . . .

. . . .

THAT'S WHAT I SEEN TODAY:

. . . .

. . . .

. . . .

THIS IS WHAT I ATE TODAY:

. . . .

. . . .

. . . .

DRAW WHAT YOU HAVE EXPERIENCED TODAY:

OR INSERT PHOTOS, ENTRY CARDS OR STAMPS

MY FAVORITE MEMORY TODAY

. . . .

. . . .

I AM GRATEFUL FOR THAT TODAY

. . . .

. . . .

THIS IS HOW MY DAY WAS TODAY

DATE: . . . .

LOCATION: . . . .

WEATHER . . . . . °F

THAT'S WHAT I EXPERIENCED TODAY:

. . . .

. . . .

. . . .

THAT'S WHAT I SEEN TODAY:

. . . .

. . . .

. . . .

THIS IS WHAT I ATE TODAY:

. . . .

. . . .

. . . .

DRAW WHAT YOU HAVE EXPERIENCED TODAY:

OR INSERT PHOTOS, ENTRY CARDS OR STAMPS

MY FAVORITE MEMORY TODAY

. . . .

. . . .

I AM GRATEFUL FOR THAT TODAY

. . . .

. . . .

THIS IS HOW MY DAY WAS TODAY

DATE: . . . .

WEATHER 🌡 . . . . °F

LOCATION: . . . .

THAT'S WHAT I EXPERIENCED TODAY:

. . . .

. . . .

. . . .

THAT'S WHAT I SEEN TODAY:

. . . .

. . . .

. . . .

THIS IS WHAT I ATE TODAY:

. . . .

. . . .

. . . .

DRAW WHAT YOU HAVE EXPERIENCED TODAY:

OR INSERT PHOTOS, ENTRY CARDS OR STAMPS

MY FAVORITE MEMORY TODAY

. . . .

. . . .

I AM GRATEFUL FOR THAT TODAY

. . . .

. . . .

THIS IS HOW MY DAY WAS TODAY

NEW FRIENDS FROM THE TRIP

FIRST NAME   NAME   STREET

. . . .

CITY   EMAIL   PHONENUMBER

. . . .

FIRST NAME   NAME   STREET

. . . .

CITY   EMAIL   PHONENUMBER

. . . .

FIRST NAME   NAME   STREET

. . . .

CITY   EMAIL   PHONENUMBER

. . . .

NEW FRIENDS FROM THE TRIP

FIRST NAME   NAME   STREET

. . . .

CITY   EMAIL   PHONENUMBER

. . . .

FIRST NAME   NAME   STREET

. . . .

CITY   EMAIL   PHONENUMBER

. . . .

FIRST NAME   NAME   STREET

. . . .

CITY   EMAIL   PHONENUMBER

. . . .

WE WOULD LIKE TO OFFER OUR PRODUCTS TO
OUR CUSTOMERS
CONSTANTLY IMPROVE.

WITH FEEDBACK IN THE FORM OF A
REVIEW, WE CAN ALSO SHARE THEIR
POSITIVE EXPERIENCES, PRAISE AND
CRITICISM CAN BE TAKEN INTO ACCOUNT.

Contact
Björn Meyer
Rönnehof 5
30457 Hannover, Germany
Override2000@gmx.de
Cover design: Björn Meyer
Design elements: vecteezy.com
www.creativefabrica.com

Made in United States
Orlando, FL
31 March 2023

31599532R00063